# 101 Essays to Empower You to Limitless Reach

Frank Agin
Founder & President
AmSpirit Business Connections



**ISBN: 978-1-967521-11-1**

**Published by:**
418 Press, A Division of Four Eighteen Enterprises LLC
Post Office Box 30724, Columbus, Ohio 43230-0724

# Acknowledgement

In sincere appreciation
of Lucas Agin.

Where do I begin?

Unpaid IT services.

Sharing time in the MCU.

YouTube laughs.

Just being you!

## Table of Contents

## Look For These Other Books in This Series

*101 Essays to Empower You to Rise & Thrive*
*101 Essays to Empower You to Up Your Game*
*101 Essays to Empower You to Build Momentum*
*101 Essays to Empower You to* Elevate Your Influence
*101 Essays to Empower You to* Peak Performance
*101 Essays to Empower You to The Winning Edge*
*101 Essays to Empower You to Live Unstoppable*
*101 Essays to Empower You to Achieve Greatness*
*101 Essays to Empower You to Break Barriers*

# Introduction

This book comes from the insight and creativity of Frank Agin.

Who is Frank? He is the founder and president of AmSpirit Business Connections, an organization that empowers entrepreneurs, sales representatives, and professionals to become successful and gain more referrals through networking.

He is the author of several books, including Foundational *Networking: Building Know, Like and Trust to Create a Lifetime of Extraordinary Success* and *The Three Reasons You Don't Get Referrals*. See all his books and programs at frankagin.com.

Finally, Frank shares information and insights on professional relationships, business networking and best practices for generating referrals on the Networking Rx podcast.

In the summer of 2018, he started planning this short-form podcast. As he mapped out what he wanted to bring to an audience of entrepreneurs, sales representatives, and professionals, he knew he'd have hundreds of programs.

But in addition to all that content, Frank noticed he also had a plethora of other materials—instructive, insightful, and inspirational. All this additional content was worthwhile, but none of it was long enough to create a full episode of Networking Rx.

Not wanting the material to go to waste, Frank developed it into short essays—approximately 150 words each. Then he started to record and share those segments daily under the brand Networking Rx Minutes.

For years, he shared a daily message of empowerment, intuition, and hope. This is a compilation of 100 of those essays. Enjoy.

## -1-
## The Hostess Mindset

According to Alison Henderson, body language expert and founder of Moving Image Consulting, one way to position yourself to get the most out of networking events is to take on the mindset of being the host.

That is, rather than attending an event hoping that others will serve you, approach the gathering as if it is your role to greet, connect and be helpful to others. In short, you would conduct yourself just as if it were a party in your own home.

The benefit of this mindset is three-fold. First, as you look to serve others, you will naturally make more and better contacts with attendees. Second, you'll be viewed by all as being gracious and helpful, drawing more people to want to be associated with you. And, finally, adopting this mindset will ensure that your body language stays open, resulting in you appearing more available and approachable.

So, at the next event, whether it's yours or not, be the hostess with the most-est.

## -2-
## The Many Flavors to Your Introduction

You might feel that there is little creativity in crafting how you introduce yourself. After all, there are only a few ways to say who you are and who you work for. And if that's all you're saying, you're no doubt right. An introduction is bland or boring.

However, when introducing yourself no one ever said you have to limit yourself to what amounts to a professional name, rank and serial number.

Prepare to move beyond the mundane. Share a little bit of what you do. And stop thinking that "There is nothing to what I do." Give yourself some credit. Think it through. There is a litany of different where's and how's to what you do.

And with that, you add dimension to your introduction by being informative or educational. Or you can really spice it up by being amusing or startling.

Your introduction is not a "vanilla or chocolate" proposition. Rather, it's like Baskin-Robins and you have 31 flavors to share.

## -3-
## Good Things in Bad

You know it. There are times in life when experiences are good and other times when they're bad. According to Be Connected author, Terry Bean, even when an experience is less than ideal, you need to learn to find the good in the bad experience.

To illustrate his point, Bean draws on the game of golf, saying: "There are 87 different ways to mess up a shot. If you look at your ball after you hit, you always find one good thing. Maybe it went 250 yards (and only 100 of them were the wrong way). Maybe it went straight as an arrow (even though it didn't go very far). Focus on that and forget the rest. Why? Because negative energy doesn't serve you well."

Bean is right. Negative energy doesn't fix anything. Rather, it generally serves to make things worse. So, with any less-than-ideal experience, find the good things in the bad and move forward to another shot.

## -4-
## Challenge the Natural Tendency

It is an all-too-common sequence of events. You devote a tremendous amount of effort to establishing some networking momentum. Things are great. You're meeting people. And things are coming from it.

Then, just as it appears your efforts will be successful, the momentum seems to dissipate for no apparent reason. And it feels as though things are sliding back to where they were. This is generally deflating and certainly frustrating.

The problem is not that you did something wrong in creating momentum. No doubt, you had a great strategy and execution. The problem, however, is that you eased your efforts too soon. As such the momentum was not sufficiently established to perpetuate itself.

Remember, it's a natural tendency to ease up when things start to move in the desired direction. Fight that urge. Don't get complacent. Double down on your game plan. While the results will never be perpetual, the momentum will become easily sustainable.

## -5-
## Giving By Giving Thanks

It was likely one of your first real life lessons: Learning to say thanks when someone does something for you. No doubt, your parents drilled this into you. And then when that became second nature, they took great pride in what you were becoming. After all, this one simple thing was the foundation to help mold you into a good citizen of the world.

While your parents knew that saying thanks was an important manner for you to master, they may not have understood the full power of this little gesture. You see, not only is it the right thing to do; saying thanks is a wonderful means of giving to others.

After all, when you take the time to say, “thank you,” you affirm the value that someone else has brought to you or the world. This, no doubt, makes them feel great as they will likely be beaming with pride. So, find every meaningful reason to thank someone.

## -6-
## What You Think About

In his book *The Power of Optimism*, corporate psychologist and motivational speaker Tim Shurr shares an important mantra: *What you think about comes about*. In fact, he feels it's so important that he writes it three times in a row.

He goes on to elaborate that our minds are hard wired to seek out what occupies it. Right now, your subconscious brain is taking in all the sights and sounds around you. As it does, it filters out the conscious things you're focused on.

So, if you think about happiness, finding great opportunities, and building wonderful relationships, then your mind will identify for you those things. And as it centers on those positives, it ignores the things that might serve to impair the uplifting energy in your life.

So, what do you want in your life? Write it down. Think about it often. In time, obviously with some effort, it will come to pass. As what you think about comes about.

## -7-
## You Get What You Commit To

A foundational law of economics is that human wants are insatiable. That is, no matter what you get or achieve, on some level you're always looking for more. There is no end to your wants.

However, a foundational law of life is that just because you want something doesn't mean you get it. In fact, want alone has never gotten anyone anything of lasting value.

Yes see, in life, when it comes to the important things, you never get what you want. You really don't. In life, the only things you can count on getting are those things that you truly commit to.

Great achievements. Wonderful victories. Amazing accomplishments. Each of these takes a level of sacrifice. All require a modicum of sustained effort. There's risk of loss, certainly in terms of time and likely an opportunity cost.

When it comes to obtaining things of lasting value, you don't get what you want. You only get what you commit to.

## -8-
## Command Your Value

You work to live. Everybody does. In exchange for your time, your talent and your toil, you're owed a compensation. After all, you earned it. You deserve it.

So, as you work, whether for a client or as an underling in some enterprise, command a fair return for your effort and guard against settling for less.

Sure, from time to time there are those who will question the value of what you offer. They might tell you it's not worth it. They might indicate they won't pay that much. So what? Think about it.

Just because someone doesn't see the value of what you offer doesn't mean that what you have to offer is worth less than the fair value you've set.

So, hold you're ground. Don't even budge a penny. Reserve your best effort for those who truly see the wonderful value that you bring.

## -9-
## We Can't Not Network

Communication consultant Felicia Slattery wrote in her book *Kill The Elevator Speech*: "As human beings, we can't not network. It's part of our nature, our collective DNA, as social beings. From caves to campfires to tribes to villages to towns to cities to social media, we are and have always been social creatures, personally and professionally."

Slattery's point is insightful. You might feel like a solitary soul, but the reality is that everything you do and everything you are, is wrapped up in the lives of the people around you. The people you serve. The people who serve you. The information upon which you rely. Everything.

You might not enjoy hob-knobbing at networking events ... and that's okay. But be sure to substitute that with other things. One-on-one meetings. Volunteering. Attending industry functions.

So, don't shrink from building relationships. In short, get up and get out of your cave, and go network. It's in your DNA.

## -10-
## Find Your Greatness

As the final whistle blew in the 2012 Ohio Division II girls state championship soccer game, the St. Francis DeSales Stallions stormed the field with screams, cheers, and a few moist eyes. The celebration was not in victory, however. No, the Stallions had just suffered the worst soccer loss in Ohio high school state championship history. Five to nothing.

Despite the loss, however, there was still much to celebrate. They'd had a great season. They'd built wonderful friendships. They'd made memories that would last a lifetime. And they'd made it further than most every other team in the state.

Though they had suffered a disappointing loss, they collected themselves, pushed past the results of one game, and took stock of all that was wonderful with their season.

This is life. Sometimes, one thing might not pan out. Despite that, there are always things for which you can celebrate. Remember, whether you meet with victory or defeat, you've achieved something. Find your greatness.

## -11-
## The Four Horsemen of Doomed Relationships

Doctors Julie and John Gottman, in working with thousands of married couples over dozens and dozens of studies, have shown that four communication styles serve to doom a relationship.

1 - Criticism: A person lodges a complaint against another that serves to attack the core of their character.

2 - Contempt: Going beyond mere criticism, a person also uses disrespect, mockery, sarcasm, ridicule, eye-rolling or scoffing to make another feel despised and worthless.

3 - Defensiveness: To deflect from their own irresponsibility or shortcoming, a person employs counter attacks, lame excuses or plays the innocent victim.

4 - Stonewalling: Rather than dealing with issues, a person withdraws from the interaction, shuts down, and simply stops responding to their partner.

The Gottmans have shown that these four behaviors serve to spell doom for most any marriage. The reality is, however, that these four horsemen have no place in any relationship, personal or professional. Don't employ them; don't allow yourself to be a victim of them.

## -12-
## Unmasking the Imposter Within

At one point or another in everyone's life there lurks a total fraud. And to spot this person all you need do is look in the mirror. In this moment, the person you see is an imposter relative to what everyone else sees. You might not feel worthy of your position. You might not feel like you're enough, relative to others.

And that's not the worst part. As Kay Coughlin, owner of Facilitator on Fire, shares: "The problem with imposter syndrome is that we get stuck in it. We peek into our own minds and see these deflating and downright depressing thoughts and we stop." Coughlin goes on to explain that you realize the issue but do nothing about it.

So, take action to unmask this imposter. Take inventory of your life and all your accomplishments. Reflect on achievements. No doubt there is a lot there. Then set about telling yourself 100 times before your head hits the pillow: "I am worthy. I am enough."

## -13-
## Good in Every Day

Have you ever had one of those days? Of course, you have. Everyone does, at one time or another.

You know. That day where nothing seems to go right. There is one misstep after another. And in trying to fix those, you get tripped up by outside forces. Whatever you do seems to take far too long. From one thing to the next there are challenges and difficulties. It's as if the world in conspiring against you. All in all, it's just one of those days.

But next time you're in one, stop. Just for a moment. And take a quick inventory of just what might not be amiss. Chances are that surrounding the things that have got you down are things for which you can be thankful. And it's more than likely that something in that day has gone right.

Yes, some days are simply not good, but there is something good in every day. When life has you down, stop to look for it.

## -14-
## The Kevin Bacon Game

Kevin Bacon is a popular American actor, linked to many of Hollywood's finest stars. So much so that it spawned a pop culture game. The idea behind the Kevin Bacon game is to link any actor to Kevin Bacon through the movies they've been in.

From this and advances of data analytics, social scientists have analyzed the connectiveness of every actor in the Internet Movie Database. What they found was that the most connected actors are not necessarily the ones who appeared in the most films. Rather the most connected actors are those who had the greatest diversity in types of movies they did, such as drama, comedy, adventure, or horror movies.

What can you take away from the Kevin Bacon game and this research? To achieve the real potential of your network, you need to operate in lots of different worlds – work, church, PTA, youth sports, trade associations, and the list goes on. In short, have a diverse life.

# -15-
# The Rainmaker's Affirmation

In his book, *The Seven Levels of Communication*, Michael Maher introduces the Rainmaker's Affirmation.

The characters in his story elaborate on this simple but powerful affirmation, that goes like this: "Each and every day, someone, somewhere in my city needs my services. My job today is to find that person."

This mantra helps to explain the difference between hard core selling and genuine networking. Hard core selling is an attempt to convince those you encounter to buy what you have. It tends to be aggressive and off-putting.

Genuine networking, however, occurs when you engage the people around you to help connect you to those they encounter who truly need what you offer.

Yes, of course, once you meet these prospective clients, you'll need to assure them that you're the person for the job and that your price and quality are aligned. But, because they have a true need, your interaction will tend to be warm and welcoming. And that makes networking a better way to do business.

## -16-
## The Wizard of Westwood

John Wooden, nicknamed the "Wizard of Westwood" was the head basketball coach at the University of California, Los Angeles." Over a 12-year period he won ten NCAA national championships, including a record seven in a row. He is arguably the most iconic and most successful college coach of all time.

Although John Wooden has quite the winning reputation, it wasn't always this way. And it didn't just happen. Prior to reaching the pinnacle of his career, he endured challenges coaching at various high schools and colleges. Even his first decade at UCLA was far less than glorious. But he stuck with it.

The simple lesson is that success in life is not necessarily easy. It is, however, somewhat formulaic. It requires you to have a large measure of hard work along with an equally sizable dose of commitment and discipline to your chosen trade, profession, or vocation. With this, success will happen. Just not overnight, or in a year, or even a decade, maybe.

# -17-
# Studied, Organized and Exciting

According to Andy Chiodo, author of *Social Capital: How to Get It, How to Use It*, "The 3 basics of successful networking are: Do your homework, be organized and be exciting."

Chiodo's advice strikes a chord. You see, some think that networking success is a matter of luck or some sort of magic that only a select few are privy to. Don't believe this. Networking success is something anyone can enjoy and it's something that everyone should aim for.

As Chiodo shares, networking success is created when:

1 - You put time in learning about the goals and aspirations of those around you. And,

2 - You organize your thoughts and intentions as to how you can help those you know. And,

3 - You carry yourself with an air of enthusiasm towards contributing to the world around you.

By being studied, organized and exciting, people are attracted to you and want to be part of your world. From there, your network flourishes.

## -18-
## 80,000 People

Eighty thousand people. That's eight and four zeroes. Brian Miller, author, speaker and TEDx magician, read that over your lifetime this is how many people you'll meet and interact with.

At first, Miller didn't believe that figure. So, he did the math. It came out to about three new people each day of your life. He didn't believe that either. So, he started to pay close attention. Soon Miller was convinced.

Then he pondered a question to himself: "Will I use those opportunities today to make my life, and the lives of the people I meet, better? The answer he had was less than positive. That became a life-changing moment, which he details in his book *Three New People*.

But you can consider that question, too. What are you doing with the people that come into your life each day? Are they just squandered opportunities? Or are you capitalizing on building new relationships? Perhaps that question can be life changing for you too.

## -19-
## Could Someone Help You

According to the book *Foundational Networking*, if you open yourself to receiving help from others, it appears that you're only getting from your network. But in an interesting sort of way, you're actually giving to it.

You see, when you allow someone to help you, you are, in essence, giving them the joy of helping you. Think about it. You give them the opportunity to experience the same elation you feel when you do things for your network.

Know this: The people in your network want to help you. They do. You help them and they want to return those wonderful deeds. They want to share with you referrals, contacts, information and meaningful opportunities.

So, today, think about and answer this question: How could someone help you? Once you seize on an idea, don't be afraid to seek that help. In so doing, you're not only receiving; you're actually contributing to your network, too.

# -20-
# Hello, My Name Is

One way to ensure that you always make a good impression on the new people you meet is to remember their name when you encounter them again.

Think about it. How do you feel when you encounter someone you've recently met, and they address you by name? No doubt, you feel as if you matter to them. Chances are, this pushes along your sense of knowing, liking and trusting them.

Knowing this, offer the same level of consideration and respect to those you've recently met. Endeavor to remember their name. Endeavor to pronounce it correctly, if it's unusual. And endeavor to know if they prefer "Michael or Mike" ... "Kimberly or Kim" ... or if it doesn't matter at all.

Remembering someone's name seems like a small inconsequential thing. In reality, however, it's a small effort that serves to have a big lasting impact. So, however you choose to remember the names of others, make it a priority. That effort will serve you well.

## -21-
## The Three Conditions of Relationship

In his acclaimed book, *Clicksand*, professional relationship expert and entrepreneur Bill Troy shares the three conditions for a relationship to exist.

First, the person needs to be someone with whom you want to have a relationship. Second, the someone needs to be open to meeting someone new. And third, you must create enough rapport with that person in order for the relationship to start and flourish.

As Troy points out, you only have control over two of these three conditions. You can be willing, and you can create rapport. However, you cannot control whether someone wants to have a relationship with you.

And that's reality. Just because there's someone new and interesting around you, doesn't mean they are ripe for you to have a relationship with. Personal or professional. And if they aren't interested, you are best to move on. Devote your time and energy to building relationships with those who are as keen about you as you are about them.

## -22-
## Have a Goal; Share a Goal

No doubt, you have goals for yourself. If you're aspiring to be more, you should. Additional professional designations. Sales targets. Career achievements. Fitness. Professional development. If you do have goals, that's great. After all, study after study has shown that people who have goals are more successful than those who don't.

But do you know what? Similar studies have also demonstrated that those who share their goals with others are far more successful than those who just have goals that they keep to themselves. Interesting, isn't it? This action seems to keep you on track.

Knowing this, doesn't it make sense to share your hopes, dreams, and aspirations with select people in your network?

While it may seem risky to do so, being vulnerable like this has the added bonus of further building your relationship with those in whom you've confided. They will rally around you. Cheer for you. And have an incentive to help you more.

So, have a goal. And share a goal with someone you know.

## -23-
## Catching Train A

Follow this word problem. Train A leaves the station at 8 o'clock going west at 50 miles per hour. Then an hour later, train B leaves the same station going in the same direction and also at 50 miles per. At what point will train B catch train A? The answer is never.

This is not a trick question. Rather, it's meant to illustrate a point. Train A represents the crowded marketplace within which you operate. There are direct competitors. There might be alternative offerings to your product or service. There's even the notion of doing without what you have to offer.

In short, no one has to hire you, and no one has to do business with you. To become relevant and capitalize on opportunities, you have to do a little more. You certainly need to be a little smarter. You need to work harder.

Train A won't wait for you to catch up. You simply must move a little faster.

## -24-
## Endless Mutual Benefits

So, what is networking, really? If you ask a dozen people, you'll likely get 12 different answers, none of which is totally right, but none are totally wrong either. So, if you want a good working definition of networking, go to an expert.

In his book, *Endless Referrals,* hall of fame professional speaker Bob Burg defines networking as "the cultivating of mutually beneficial, give-and-take, win-win relationships."

Burg hits all the important points. Networking is a cultivation. It's not simply a harvest. But rather it's also a tilling, a planting and tending to.

Networking is mutually beneficial, give-and-take, win-win. It's not a grab what you can and move on. Rather it's a back and forth, help and be helped scenario.

And networking is about relationships. It's not a singular transaction at some moment in time. Rather, it's an ongoing, seemingly endless interaction with others.

Networking is truly "the cultivating of mutually beneficial, give-and-take, win-win relationships."

## -25-
## Don't Interrupt

What are some ways you can guard against interrupting others? Bite your tongue? Consciously, keep your lips pursed? Become uber focused on what the others person is saying and how they say it?

Whatever you need to do to prevent yourself from interrupting someone else, do it. Why? Because, obviously, if you are interrupting you are not listening very well – you are focused on what you are going to say.

No doubt, you have something insightful and important to add. It might even be funny and highly entertaining. However, the reality is that to build a solid vibrant network, you need to be a proficient listener.

Remember great networking involves adding value to others. And you cannot begin to add value to those in your network unless and until you know what they need or want.

So, be a great networker. Zip it and listen.

## -26-
## The Tale of Two Prides

Motivational speaker and organizational consultant Simon Sinek shares that there are two types of pride.

One is authentic, where you exhibit a positive but proportionate sense of your self-worth. You gain respect through your efforts, but you're confident enough in yourself to give credit to others when its due. When you exhibit authentic pride, you motivate others to achieve, and they rally around what you're looking to achieve.

The second type of pride tends to be arrogant and narcissistic. Those exhibiting this pride gain power through fear and bullying others and via behavior that is best described as aggressive and rude. They don't achieve anything of substance via their own hard work or good intentions. Rather they accomplish much from hijacking the accolades due to another or basking in the positive reflection someone else has cast.

What pride do you aspire to? Take action today so that you move in that direction.

# -27-
# "Throwing A Dart" Networking

An important aspect of successful networking is knowing what to do. However, also important is knowing what not to do in building a network.

In his book, *Who Do You Need To Meet?*, networking maven Rob Thomas shares:

"Some who network treat it like a numbers game. They gather a pile of business cards that they add to their growing pile of faceless names and forgotten intentions. This is what I call 'throwing a dart' networking. Maybe you will magically score, but typically you won't."

As Thomas implies, your networking efforts should not be the equivalent of pitching sharp objects at a board and hoping something hits just right. His foundational principle of networking is that the lifeline of business are relationships, and those relationships are between people. Those relationships are not built through mass e-mails that amount to meaningless follow up. Rather they are formed person by person, one at a time.

## -28-
## The Value of Expertise

There's a cute parable that goes something like this: A family has a stair that gives out a deafening creak whenever they step on it. Determined to rid their house of this annoying quirk, they contact an old, neighborhood handyman.

The handyman comes in. Steps on the stair once. Creak. Then twice. Creak. He takes a close-up look, then without a word pulls out a two-inch finish nail and proceeds to hammer it into the step with three solid taps.

He steps on the stair again. Once. No sound. Twice. Silence. Three times. Nothing.

The family is amazed. As each of them tests the stair, they are completely astonished. They are equally astonished, however, when the handyman gives them the bill.

The father remarks in disbelief, "$100 for a minute of your time and one nail!" To which the old handyman replies, "Yes! One cent for the nail and $99.99 for knowing where to put it."

Remember, your value is less about time and more about expertise.

# -29-
# Achieving Lifelong Success

The formula for lifelong success is simple. Get up every day and work to achieve something of value. Yes, it's that simple.

It's true. Lifelong success is the achievement of an almost endless succession of objectives. You get through kindergarten, move through grade school, and get your high school diploma. Then it's off to college or to hone a vocation. From there, enter the workforce or start a business and it continues. And every day you gain a little more status.

Every day, you endeavor to move forward, gaining ground in life that you never intend to give back. You hone your expertise and that creates value. You read things and that enhances knowledge. You listen to others and that creates wisdom. And, you work hard and that builds status.

Lifelong success is about stepping forward metaphorically, day after day. It is truly a journey. So, embrace every step of the way.

## -30-
## Responding to 'Thank You'

If you're engaged in the world as you should be, no doubt you're providing value to others. Kudos! That's great. As part of that, others will express their gratitude in some form or fashion, usually by saying thanks.

As John Millen shared in his blog post, *How To Respond To Thank You*, when someone says "thanks," you can actually do yourself a disservice by sloughing off your efforts as "no big deal." Relying on academic research, he encourages you to use this as an opportunity to make someone feel special.

So next time someone thanks you, rather than saying "no problem," go with "Your relationship is important to us, so I was happy to do this for you."

Or, rather than going with "Just doing my job," say "You know, your friendship means a lot, so I really wanted to go the extra mile for you."

Again, make those who thank you feel special, and you'll find yourself with more opportunities.

## -31-
## Trees and Sunlight

From the moment a tree seedling germinates and bursts through the ground, it's committed to one thing. Growth. Day after day, it embarks on this never-ending mission.

It takes in sunlight to fuel this expansion, working itself upward. Reaching and reaching. And in its desires to continue, it drives itself outward seeking more sunlight. Expanding and expanding.

To be all you can, you need to be much like the tree. From the moment you burst into the professional world you must commit to ongoing growth. And the sunlight to fuel this growth is knowledge and experience.

You need to seek more knowledge relevant to your professional world by reaching and reaching for information, insights and ideas that can push you forward. At the same time, you must pursue experiences that challenge you and help you expand your confidence and capabilities.

To be truly successful long-term, you need to be like a tree. Reach for knowledge. And expand yourself through experiences.

## -32-
## Opportunities in Every Contact

It is easy to do, and everyone is guilty of it at one time or another. That is dismissing someone in your mind as being of little or no consequence to you. Maybe it was a gas station attendant. Maybe it was a receptionist. Maybe it was the person delivering the paper.

Know this, however. While everyone may not be your next prospective client, everyone knows someone that might be. No, not everyone will fit neatly into your network as a center of influence, but everyone is connected to someone who could. Of course, not everyone is going to be chock full of useful information, but you can bet they sure know a person who is.

Knowing this, everyone deserves and should receive the respect and attention that you would offer your best clients, centers of influence, or prime information sources. Remember, within every encounter, there lies opportunity.

# -33-
# Your Ally, Pressure

Lots of things go into success. One, however, that is seldom mentioned is pressure. To achieve anything, you need to take your abilities to that edge. You know. The one where the situation makes you sit up straight, focus a bit more, and your heart gets racing. It makes you feel alive. If you avoid this sensation, you risk getting stuck in mediocrity.

In his book, *The Next One Up Mindset*, mental edge guru Grant Parr shares, "If we learn to prepare and train our minds, we too can come to love pressure and use it to our advantage. After all, we mostly create our own pressure."

Parr is right. Everyone creates their own pressure. The difference is that some allow it to cripple them. Others use it to catapult them forward. If you want success bad enough, learn to have pressure be a catapult for you. Learn to love it. Embrace it. Make pressure your ally, not an enemy.

## -34-
## A Rookie Back-Up

Jacob Givens really wanted to play hockey for his high school, the Hancock Bulldogs in Michigan's Upper Peninsula.

Unfortunately, competition was stiff. As a result, Givens failed to make the team his freshman and sophomore years. And that was likely going to be the case his junior year as well. You see, the team was fully stocked with veteran players at his position.

Nevertheless, Givens really wanted to be a Bulldogs hockey player. So, he did something unconventional. He did something he really didn't want to do. He tried out and made the team as a goalie, as the team only had one other person at that position.

And because of this, one weekend he had a chance to shine. You see, when the starting keeper was injured, Givens stepped in, provided a heroic effort, and helped the Bulldogs defeat two top-ranked opponents. The lesson is simple: In life, often to do the things you want, you have to do the things you don't.

## -35-
## Lose the Sight of Shore

For centuries, sailors whisked around the oceans and seas, with the shoreline clearly insight. While there were still risks, this vocation offered them an exceptional livelihood relative to their “land-bound” contemporaries. Despite this, seldom did any of these sailors ever achieved great fame or fortune.

A select few, however, were not content with hugging the coast. Rather, they were endowed with an uncommon courage that inspired them to venture out. Push beyond the horizon. And lose the sight of shore.

Because of this exploration, these brave sailors became rich and have gone down in history as discovering new oceans, fruitful lands, and interesting people.

Today, the same rules apply. There is a decent living working hard and playing it safe. But the real fame and fortune go to those willing to venture out and do something bold. If you want to discover that new ocean, whatever that might be, you need to have the courage to lose sight of shore.

## -36-
## The Never-Ending Battle

Here's a reality: You cannot control your subconscious mind. Sensations whip in and out. And it processes hundreds and hundreds of bits of information every moment of every day.

Although you lack control over these unconscious feelings, you're not completely helpless. As Steve Gutzler, consultant and author of *Emotional Intelligence for Personal Leadership*, shares, "There is a 24/7 battlefield for your mind — your thoughts. Be intentional, control your thoughts and what you put in mind."

No, you have no control over the internal workings of your mind and what subliminal cues it takes from the world. You do, however, have complete control over what you put into it. You can choose to fill your mind with positive thoughts and aspirations. You can choose to associate with uplifting people. You can choose what you listen to and read. And you can choose to rationalize away dark thoughts.

There is a never-ending battle within your mind. Do all you can to allow positivity to win.

## -37-
## Stone Soup Networking

In the tale, *Stone Soup*, stingy villagers have no interest in sharing their food with anyone but their own.

However, when a peddler offers to share some stone soup with them (essentially rocks in a pot of boiling water), one by one, the villagers begin to share - a head of cabbage here, some salt beef there - and before long a pot of delicious "stone" soup awaits them.

This tale suggests that generosity and altruism are contagious. And many social science experiments have demonstrated that this is true. But people don't just give; they are somehow moved and inspired to do so.

The takeaway is that you have the power to inspire generosity in others through your own generosity. Any simple gesture can be contagious – a simple referral, an introduction, or just sharing valuable information. This will inspire your network to give. Give to you. Give to others. And create generosity that cascades forward across time.

## -38-
## A Referral Machine

No doubt, you are ambitious. And you absolutely want to be more successful. Right?

But you're savvy too. You know that the road to greater success is not merely a brute force effort of working longer and harder. No, you know it's about working smarter.

You know you need a sales force. You know, a core of people who are working for you even when you're not working.

And, in reality, you've already got this. Your network. These are friends, colleagues, strategic partners, and even former clients sending you prospective clients. These individuals are essentially a referral machine.

After all, referrals are the most effective means of creating long-term, sustainable success. Moreover, it's the best place to be in business ... any business or any profession. At this point, your new clients are almost exclusively generated from people in your network. That's where you want to be, right?

So, ask yourself, "What am I doing today to create this referral machine?"

## -39-
## Happy People Create

Christine Schlonski, an internationally renowned consultant, and host of the Heart Sells podcast, has a firm belief: "If hurt people, hurt people ... happy people create happy people."

It doesn't take much imagination to realize that Schlonski's theory is valid. When you're happy, you cannot help but have that happiness spill over into the lives of others. Your family. Your friends. Co-workers. Colleagues. And clients. When you're happy, others get swept up in that elation.

And because you're sharing your happiness, you've brought something wonderful into the lives of others. After all, life is seldom easy. In fact, many days it's downright difficult. That's what makes the joy you contribute so special. As a result, others are drawn to you, hopeful that you will bring some sunshine into their world.

Knowing this, make being happy a priority. Look for the good in others. Look for the positive in life. Find any and every reason to smile. Remember, Schlonski's words: happy people create happy people.

## -40-
## A Network Building Tool

Far too often, people figuratively chain themselves to their computer and clank away in LinkedIn, Facebook or Twitter hoping to create business for themselves. While they may stumble onto some, it seldom reaches the level they hope for.

Know this: social media is not a sales machine. It is not an order-taking system. It is not an ATM. It is merely a tool that you can use to better network yourself. And by no means is it a replacement for networking.

Think about it. We networked before we had telephones. This invention just allowed us to connect faster and further. But the telephone itself was just a tool.

The same is true of social media. It is just a tool. It is not networking. It is just a tool to make it easier to get to know people, determine if we like them, and then ultimately trust them. Don't hope social media is your network. Rather use it to build your network.

## -41-
## Hard Work Beats Talent

Forgotten in history are the names and stories of incredibly talented people who never applied themselves. In fact, nowhere in the annals of time is the tale of someone who rode talent alone to fame and fortune.

Sure, there have been talented people. William Shakespeare. Isaac Newton. Ben Franklin. Steve Jobs. And the list goes on and on. While each is known for a wonderful talent, ability, idea or insight, seldom mentioned in their run-up to distinction is the time and toil they invested in their so-called craft.

But if you really examined the lives of this lot of achievers, you'd find that coupled with their amazing talents was a commitment to applying themselves. Daily long hours. Week after week. Year after year. Grinding. Thinking. Practicing. Exploring ideas and concepts. Working through notions.

Remember this: Hard work is far more important than talent, especially when the talented don't work hard.

## -42-
## Birthday Card Revival

As professional speaker Matt Ward shares in his book *MORE: Word of Mouth Referrals, Lifelong Customers and Raving Fans*, "Celebrating birthdays is as simple as a few clicks." But he also reminds us that everyone knows (as you do) that the 200 people who recognize them on their special day, did so using the path of least resistance.

Ward offers this idea instead. When celebrating birthdays, he challenges us to do so in a throwback sort of way. Rather than the path of least resistance, send an actual birthday card.

Yes, it takes a little more effort to pick out a card and label an envelope. And yes, there is a little bit of an expense purchasing a card and stamp. And no, sending a birthday card is not an innovative idea. That has been done for years.

But what Ward advocates is more of a revival that will keep you top of mind with everyone you really want to matter.

## -43-
## Valuing Your Network

You need to view your network as more than just people with whom you interact. You need to view it for what it is – an asset. Just like a share of company stock or a piece of land.

After all, just as these various assets contribute to your total net worth, every contact you have and every relationship you build also contributes to aspects of your wealth. You see, contacts and relationships build your social capital.

Though not necessarily in dollars and cents, this asset serves as an approximate valuation as to how those you interact with enhance your life, both personally and professionally. It is your ability to use your network to get information, new clients, or another job.

So how much social capital do you have? Do you ever think about it?

After all, you account for the money you have in the bank, right? Why not put some consideration into the one thing that helped you get it there?

## -44-
## Grow Or Shrink Relationships

Peter Drucker, famed author, educator, and management consultant, whose writings contributed to practical foundations of the modern business corporation, once remarked, "A business either grows, or it shrinks. It doesn't stand still."

Drucker's mantra is insightful. Given the options, the choice is obvious. If you're in business, you need to commit to ongoing growth. After all, why would you submit to having your endeavors dwindle away.

While Drucker's quote clearly applies to business, it applies to networking as well. Think about it. A relationship either grows and improves, or it's prone to atrophy. There is no middle ground where things just stand still.

So, with everyone you know, that's the choice. Build and reinforce your connection. Or sit by and let it slip away. Given that option, what do you want to do? With the people who are important to you, commit to the relationship. Invest time. Put forth energy. Continue to build on it.

## -45-
## Like First; Be Liked Second

"It's hard to say 'No' to a friend," influence consultant Brian Ahearn reminds us in his book *Influence People*. He alternatively shares "that people prefer to say, 'Yes' to those they know and like." With this insight, you should devote much energy to getting people to like you.

While this might not be a revelation, what Ahearn shares next will be: "Too often people are concerned with doing whatever it takes to get people to like them, failing to realize if they genuinely liked the person first, that individual will sense it and naturally reciprocate."

So, to get people to like you, devote your energy to finding ways to like them. For example, look for what you have in common. Or give them genuine compliments. And even find ways to work together with them cooperatively.

If you want to establish quick rapport with those you've met, make it a habit to like them first. You'll be liked in return.

## -46-
## I'm Sorry, But I Forgot Your Name

Here's the scenario. You're at an event and you encounter someone you recently met at another event. It's great to see them again, but ... wouldn't you know it ... you forgot their name.

While this is not ideal, it happens. And to most everyone. So, there is no transgression in not remembering. The potential sin, however, is carrying on as if you did.

Sure, you can fake it. And it might seem homey to fallback to something like "Buddy or Friend." In reality, this networking ruse is nothing short of disingenuous.

While you serve to establish rapport when you remember the name of someone you recently met, don't despair it you happen to forget. When you do, simply own it and say something like, "It's great to see you again, but I'm embarrassed to say that I can't remember your name." Truth be told, this honesty will heighten that person's appreciation for you.

## -47-
## The Leading Impression

Upon meeting, one of the first things people use to form an opinion about you is your business card. Right or wrong, that little piece of thin cardstock creates a leading impression about who you are, what you do, and even how well you do it.

For this reason, make an investment in your business cards. Enlist the services of a designer to craft a logo that's appropriate for you. And then have them work it into a sharp looking layout that serves to represent you long after you depart from an encounter.

From here, do NOT skimp on its production. Don't generate these tiny billboards by running thin, perforated cardstock through your laser printer. Rather, find a quality printer. And then have this professional make up on hardy cardstock 500 to a 1,000 business cards.

Remember, your business card is your leading impression. So, approach its design and production that way.

## -48-
## Borrowed Trust

Renowned speaker, author, and business networking expert Bill Cates shares in his book, *Beyond Referrals*, that "People don't do business with us – or give us referrals – until they trust us. Therefore, we want to meet all our new prospects starting at the highest point of trust."

Cates goes on to share that this highest point is when the introduction is facilitated by someone who the person we're meeting already trusts. In essence, he remarks, "We borrow the trust of one relationship long enough to earn our own trust in the new relationship."

The implication for Cates' notion of borrowed trust is that you should avoid asking people to send business your way. And you should refrain for asking for referrals. Rather, you should become laser focused on the types of people you want to have in your professional life. Then, start asking the people who trust you to introduce you to the people they know that fit the clear image in your mind.

## -49-
## Laughter Lightens the Load

In an interview, comedian Kevin Hart shared, "Laughter heals all wounds, and that's one thing that everybody shares. No matter what you're going through, it makes you forget about your problems. I think the world should keep laughing."

Certainly, Hart is in the business of laughter and arguably he's very adept at his craft. And while his craft might not be yours, no one says that you can't use humor to give you a leg up in creating relationships.

Think about it. Life is not easy. Even the most successful among us struggle with problems and challenges. And while a cute one-liner or a small cartoon shared out of the newspaper won't make those go away, the shared humor will serve to lighten the moment. Bring forth a smile. Maybe even elicit a little chuckle.

While this probably won't get you a gig on the stand-up comedy circuit, it will likely bring you a little close to the professional gig you're after.

## -50-
## The Anatomy of 30-Seconds

To build a strong network of connections that give you referrals, contacts, and information, you need to have a concise, yet very compelling, 30-second commercial. The problem is that you have so much to say, and 30 seconds is really not a lot of time.

So, to conquer this challenge, here's an effective framework to work with.

Start with a 5-second basic introduction that addresses the "who" you are, such as your name and the business you represent.

Add to that a message that addresses the "what you do" in 15 seconds or less;

From there, use 5-seconds to create credibility by sharing how long you've been doing it or some key clients you've served.

Finally, wrap this up with a 5-second, strong definite request as to how they might help you.

Now, if you carefully draft each of these sub-parts and then piece them together with your own personal flair, you end up with a very effective 30-second commercial. Good luck.

## -51-
## The Spirit of Connectiveness

Being effectively networked, in time, becomes less about constantly meeting new people and infinitely more about staying in contact with those you already know. This notion, however, generally conjures up sentiments like, "What is it that I'm saying to all these people?" Or "I don't want to bother these people."

Marketing consultant Kimberly Rice shares an appropriate response to this in her book *Rainmaker Roadmap*: "Reach out with a helpful spirit and the true intention of checking in."

As Rice implies, offer your assistance, however they might need it, even if it's not connected to what you do professionally. "Checking in" can be related to business transactions or starting a new position at work. But it can also relate to things that are more personal in nature, such as remembering milestones or noting family happenings, such as graduations, vacations, or other activities.

Staying in contact is really less about the topic and more about the spirit that moves you.

## -52- Transitioning On

Attending networking events is important. So is knowing what to do once you get there. Like, being adept at entering a conversation, making small talk, and then, eventually, moving on.

It's true. While it's important to be good at carrying a conversation, it's equally important to learn how to wrap one up and transition to someone new.

After all, it wouldn't make sense to spend all your time at an event talking to one person. So, here are some ideas on how you can move from one good conversation to another:

"Thanks for your time. I told myself I would meet three interesting people today. I have two more to go."

Or "There is someone over there that I need to connect with. Let's get together soon."

Or "Is there anyone here in particular you would like to meet? I would be glad to introduce you."

Any one of these can help you artfully move out of one conversation and set you up to start another.

## -53-
## Fishing For Others

The best way to get opportunities from your network – such as, new clients or additional business – is to provide opportunities to it.

While it might seem daunting, finding opportunity for others is not as challenging as it might seem. In many respects, it's like fishing and involves only three steps. Bait. Cast. Reel.

One. Bait the hook. That is, identify features associated with the people, products and services within your network that could be potentially beneficial to others. Then ...

Two. Cast the baited hooks, which is to tastefully share information about those features with those in your network who could benefit. And finally ...

Three. Reel in the catch. Once someone expresses an interest in the benefit, this is the opportunity to connect them to the person who can help.

And unlike actual fishing, when you fish for opportunities for others, no catch is too small. Every opportunity is a keeper.

## -54-
## Super Networker Secret

Do you want to know a secret to great networking? Here's one from consultant Jason Treu from his book *Social Wealth*: "Meeting people in groups or organizations is the fastest and most efficient way to accumulate and manage your social capital and is the least resource intensive. This is the secret that super networkers use to consistently meet a lot of new people."

Treu goes on to share that through groups and organizations there is a heightened degree of immediate trust. As a result, the exchange of referrals, contacts, and information is more free flowing. And the association with like-minded individuals allows you to be more open, direct, vulnerable, authentic, honest, and giving. This results in you being able to more rapidly convert mere interactions into true relationships.

Knowing all of this, you should have every incentive to find a group or organization that fits you well. Then become involved with it as if your networking depends on it. Because it does.

## -55-
## Looking For Base Hits

Networking is about helping others and then trusting that in time they will help you in return. By that definition, it starts with you. You need to take the initiative in doing for others and you need to become patient in waiting for those efforts to come back to you.

When the attention turns to you and others ask how they can help you, don't get consumed asking for "game changing" opportunities. You know, the game winning "home runs". While these are wonderful, they tend to be very few and far between. And unless your network has one readily in sight, they will quickly stop trying to find one.

Rather focus your requests on little things. Things that are of benefit and relatively easy to find. These "base hits" might not be exciting. Over time, however, one by one these seemingly mundane acts serve to collectively move the needle. And in the end, this strategy will be most productive for you.

## -56-
## The Highest Compliment

The best compliment that you can receive has nothing to do with your intelligence or insight. It has nothing to do with what you achieve or how hard you work. The greatest compliment you can receive is that you are reliable.

Why? It's simple. Reliability is the foundation upon which all our talents and characteristics rest.

Reliability is everything. A great work ethic will get you nowhere unless you do what you say. Wonderful insight or superior intellect is critically handicapped by an inability to honor your word. Reliability goes to the heart of establishing others' trust in you.

So, if someone says you are being smart, say thanks. If they call you a hard worker, nod in appreciation. If you are told you've got great insight, smile in gratitude.

But if someone says they can depend on you, then do all three. Because when they do, they're indicating you are reliable. And that the highest compliment of all.

## -57-
## Dreams Plus Goals Equals Vision

As speaker and personal development influencer Lewis Howes reminds in his book, *The School of Greatness*, "A powerful vision emerges when we couple our dreams with a set of clear goals."

As Howes implies, there is nothing wrong with dreams, but without goals your ability to live those dreams is impaired. And goals are great, if not vital. But if you don't have them tied to an underlying dream, the inspiration to see your goals through will be lacking.

Without both a dream and the goals to achieve it, Howes states, "you are apt to wander in a clueless and purposeless fog."

Don't get stuck in this state. Stop to envision the dreams you have for yourself, both personally and professionally. Then attach to those dreams clear and realistic goals. After all, the dreams will fuel your efforts with purpose. And your goals will provide clues as to how you can see them through.

## -58-
## Eleven Seconds to Courage

Growing up, Travis Roy had one goal: To play Division I college hockey like his father. In the fall of 1995, his dreams were realized as he enrolled at Boston University on a scholarship to play hockey for the Terriers.

Unfortunately, 11 seconds into the first shift of his collegiate career, Roy took an odd fall headlong into the boards, cracking his fourth and fifth cervical vertebra. This paralyzed him from the neck down. His college career and hockey dream were over.

However, he vowed that it would not end his life. Roy went on to graduate from Boston University in four years. He became an author. He became a sought-after motivational speaker. And he became a tireless advocate for people with spinal cord injuries.

Travis Roy's story offers a lesson. Yes, life will hand you setbacks. It might even give you tragedies to deal with. Despite that, don't stop forging ahead and making a great impact on the world.

## -59-
## Dating 101

Imagine this: You've got a daughter who's been asked out on a date. The date arrives a few minutes late, toots the horn and expects her to run out to the car. Then she has another date with someone else. This person arrives a tad early and comes up to the door with flowers, candy, and a willingness to meet you. Here's the question: Who do you encourage her to go out with again?

The answer is almost rhetorical. You can see when people are being treated well and when they're not. You know when you're being treated well and when you're not. You simply need to keep that in mind as you interact with others.

It's no big secret, but if you look to build strong, long-term relationships, you need to treat those in your network in a fashion that will make them want to connect with you again and again.

## -60-
## Slow Down to Speed Up

In his book, *A Life Best Lived*, master business coach Danny Creed shares a counterintuitive insight: "There is an old Zen teaching that says in order to be successful, we must slowdown in order to speed up."

Creed goes on to explain that often you become your own worst enemy by continuing to do what you've been doing. By taking the time, however, to slow down and refrain from the constant grind, perhaps just a half a step, you can honestly analyze what you've been doing.

From this slower pace you gain an understanding and acceptance that what you're doing is either not effective or, worse yet, actually undermining your efforts.

With this insight, you can alter your course or tweak your approach. From there, you can not only get back the half of step you lost but also pick up the pace going forward. As Creed implies, often the best way to speed up is to slow down first.

## -61-
## Build On Relationships

You know lots of people. You do. Think about it. In fact, chances are, you know more people now than you could possibly meet over the next year, maybe two. You know people in your community. You know people from high school, college, and your career.

So, while meeting new people is always an important part of networking, remember there is a tremendous advantage to networking with familiar names and faces. What is it? These people already have a relationship with you. And that is a wonderful head start to productive and effective networking. All you need to do is capitalize on it.

Given that, focus energy on connecting with the people you already know and reconnecting with old friends and acquaintances. Get caught up on their lives. Think of ways you can help them. Share with them about your professional endeavors. And remember to ask for assistance.

In short, build on the relationships you already have.

# -62-
# I Apologize

Do you think that saying you're sorry makes you appear weak? If so, you'd be wrong.

In that moment, no doubt you're vulnerable. You've surrendered yourself to another, admitting you're flawed and that somehow that harmed them. And, mostly importantly, you've revealed that you feel bad and will endeavor for it to never happen again.

The curious thing about this vulnerability, however, is that it ultimately elevates you in the eyes of others. Think about it. This act of contrition – facing a client, friend or employee and saying, "I am truly sorry" – is not an easy thing to do. It takes tremendous courage. And this courage will earn you a heightened level of respect in the eyes of others. In short, this will bolster how people come to know, like and trust you.

So never be afraid to say, "I apologize." This statement is more aligned with demonstrating your strength and self-confidence than exposing any sort of weaknesses.

# -63-
# Casting a Positive Stone

During the 2019 TEDx program in Detroit, co-organizer Terry Bean briefly took the stage. In the allotted few minutes, he shared this one big idea: We all have the ability to cast a positive stone, creating ripples that benefit others.

In addition, he also shared these eight ideas for casting positive stones.

1. Hold the door for someone.
2. Celebrate important milestones with the people you love.
3. Smile, or better yet, make someone else smile.
4. Lend an ear by being there for those who need you.
5. Shine the light on people doing excellent work.
6. Pay it forward with something as simple as buying someone a cup of coffee.
7. Connect the people you know with the people they need to know. And,
8. Be kind.

Bean's list is not just a simple one; it's also a list of little things that you can do each and every day to create positive ripples in the world.

## -64-
## Why You?

Everyone has competition. Everyone, including you. Knowing this, it begs the question: What makes you unique amongst your competition?

Think about it. This question is important. And your answer to it has lots of important implications. Like, how does a customer or client select you in a crowded marketplace?

So, know the answer as to "why you?" Is it price? That is, is the cost of what you offer lower than anyone else? Is it quality? Is there something about what you have that is more durable or better refined or some other characteristic that creates real and lasting value? Is there a patented technology, proprietary process or specialized education or background? Is there something that the others can't readily duplicate?

So, why you? Whatever it is or however you define it, you need an answer to that question. Moreover, you need to be ready to communicate it in a clear, concise and confident fashion.

## -65-
## Stopping Bad Men

Ignore what you hear on the news. Skip past what's printed on page one of your paper. The world has much to be optimistic about. There are initiatives looking to tackle disease, poverty, literacy, and you name it. The world is really headed in the right direction.

It is, however, far from perfect. There are still those who have malicious intent. There are those whose motives are anything but pure. And there are those who are misguided in both word and deed. As they maneuver, however, don't sit idly by and accept it. As 19th century British philosopher, political economist, and civil servant John Stuart Mill warned:

"Bad men need nothing more to compass their ends than that good men should look on and do nothing."

Don't do nothing. Speak up. Notify someone. Organize a resistance. Take a stand. Be courageous. Confirm the situation. In short, do your part to make the world – even just your corner of it – a better place.

## -66-
## Managing the Inbox

In the December 2019 issue of Success Magazine, Tony Jeary (aka The Results Guy) provided an answer to this question: How you can become more efficient when it comes to managing your email inbox. After working with the largest companies and top achievers, his best advice is this:

1 - Leverage the subject line. That is, if the message can be conveyed in that area, do so.

2 - Get it good enough and get it out. Too often people labor over every word and punctuation mark of a message. Remember, generally it's just an e-mail and not a business proposal. It doesn't need to be perfect. It just needs to convey information. And,

3 - Use the phone to avoid too much back and forth. There are times when five minutes talking can replace a half-dozen e-mail volleys. Become attuned to when this is the case and pick up the phone instead. It's a time saver.

## -67-
## The Fiesta Fake Out

In 2009, Dane Ebanez walked onto the University of Oregon football team with little expectation of ever playing in a game. After all, he was only 5'9" and weighed a modest 180 pounds.

Despite being virtually anonymous, Ebanez was an active member of the team. He attended hundreds of film sessions and practices. He toiled day in and day out on the scout team. He spent hours studying and executing plays of Oregon's opponents.

And, while Ebanez thought no one noticed his efforts, someone did. In 2013 when Oregon had the Fiesta Bowl in hand, a teammate who knew of his commitment, ensured Ebanez's hard work was rewarded. He found an opportunity for the walk-on to slip into the game for one play.

The lesson is this: Work hard at whatever you do. And find opportunities to sacrifice, even if you think no one is noticing. Chance are, someone is. And your reward is coming.

## -68-
## Fear Can't Have You

Life is full of unknowns. Every day brings new challenges to conquer. Every day brings strangers into your life. Every day there is something that you haven't dealt with before.

No one knows what tomorrow will bring. No one. And that can be scary.

And do you know what? It's okay to be afraid. It's okay to feel a bit of apprehension churning in your gut. It's okay to have a little bit of fear.

But what's not okay is allowing fear to have you. It's not okay to let this anxiety well up so much inside you that it paralyzes you from taking action on pursuing your hopes and dreams. It's not okay to allow fear to keep you from making the unknown known.

If you sense fear ... when you sense fear, face up to it. Stare it down. And then move through it, whatever it is. Fear can't have you.

## -69-
## Top Ten Happiness Habits

Happy people have more vibrant networks than their brooding counterparts. This makes sense. An upbeat demeanor literally draws people to you. Given that it begs the question, what are the most powerful habits to boost your happiness?

Dr. John Schinnerer, relationship consultant and host of the Evolved Caveman Podcast, maintains that happiness can be boiled down to learned skills. He then reveals that according to science, the top ten happiness habits are:

1. Be kind to others.
2. Be mindful.
3. Savoring the world around you.
4. Learning new things.
5. Having meaningful goals.
6. Practicing.
7. Exhibiting positive emotions.
8. Finding meaning and purpose to your life.
9. Exhibiting compassion for oneself and others, and
10. Maintaining positive relationships.

The benefits of happiness are extensive, especially to building your network and getting there is not difficult, at all. Why not start now? After all, the habits on Doctor Schinnerer's list are things you can start building today.

## -70-
## Building Referral Partners

If you're in business, you know that referrals are the most cost-effective source of revenue. And you know to build referral partners into your business strategy, you need to establish relationships. This then begs the question: "With whom should I establish these relationships? "

No doubt, you're open to accepting referrals from anyone. And you should be. But you can't have a referral-generating relationship with everyone. So, you need to be tactical about it.

Try this: First, articulate in your mind the profile of the potential great clients you'd like to have. Then list out all those professionals who are likely of service to these potential clients. Boom! These are the people with whom you want to create a relationship. Why? They're strategic partners. After all, they operate in the circles where you want to operate, but don't compete with you. Thus, their clients could be good clients for you. Think about it.

## -71-
## The Power of Dreams

Gold medal Olympian, hurdler and humanitarian, Wilma Rudolph, once remarked, "Never underestimate the power of dreams and the influence of the human spirit. The potential for greatness lives within each of us."

What Rudolph was driving at is that no matter who you are, no matter where you came from, or no matter where you are right now, you have every ability to be something more.

She's right. You have the potential to advance your life. You can be operating at a higher plateau. You can be that much closer to greatness. But it starts with your vision for yourself.

Don't be afraid to dream. Don't be afraid to long for something more. Don't be afraid to close your eyes and envision what your potential can be. Yes, achieving things will involve much more, but you can't get started without a dream.

## -72-
## Out Of the Mindset Slump

Dr. Rob Bell, podcast host and sports psychologist offers three ways to upgrade your mindset and pull out of the funk of feeling bad about yourself.

One, change your environment. Whether it's a full-on vacation, a mini stay-cation or simply changing where you sit, altering your environment can serve to provide a mental health re-boot.

Two, evaluate your relationships. Actively build into your life relationships with people who "get you"; people who, no matter what, make you feel good about yourself. And,

Three, hang out with winners. Bell makes the point that in baseball dugouts those hitting well hang out with others who are hitting well. Metaphorically, who's hitting well in your life? Get in their dugout. Remember, you are the average of the five people closest to you. So, make sure your environment breeds success and supports you!

Any (or all) of these tips will get you out of the mindset slump.

## -73-
## Keep Moving

Why do you go to networking events? Simple. To meet new people and reconnect with those you already know. So, when you're at these events, to maximize the effectiveness of your "meet and reconnect" mission, don't stay too long in one place or with one person.

If you stay too long in one place, you're at the mercy of the natural flow of the event. If you move about, you control where you are and when you get there.

If you linger too long with one person, you risk exhausting a relationship before it gets going. Plus, you lose out of the other potential relationships around the event.

So, here's the plan. Meet someone. Strike up a good conversation. Exchange business cards. Then, after ten minutes or so, excuse yourself with a pleasantry such as, "It was nice meeting you ... there are a couple other people I need to talk with today." Then move on.

## -74-
## Build A Bridge

Where would the world be without bridges? You know, those wood or steel structures that serve to connect two things. Without bridges, on a distant shore there would be a great many strangers. Without bridges, lots of roads would dead end at the water's edge. Without bridges, lives would be tethered to ferries bringing them to and fro.

But bridges are not just physical structures. Bridges are also connections. They are connections you create between yourself and another person. They are connections you create between two people that don't know each other. They are connections you create between ideas or information and the need for insight.

And just as the world is better with physical bridges, it's also better because of the bridges you create amongst people, information and opportunities. On the road to success, these bridges are everything. So, take a little time today to build a bridge. It's the quickest path to lasting success.

## -75-
## Goal Sharing

There is little argument that goal setting is vital to success. It works in sports. It works in business. It works relative to personal finances. Goals are the road to achievement.

But often overlooked, and certainly underappreciated, is goal sharing. As sports psychologist Grant Parr shares in his book, *The Next One Up Mindset*:

"You need to be willing to share your goals with others. To tell your friends and family, coaches and bosses about them so that there will be someone else out there who will help hold you accountable. Without accountability, goals are meaningless."

Parr offers sage advice. Having a goal is great. But its complete and total effectiveness only happens when you have the courage to let someone else know about it. With that simple act, you become vulnerable, to be sure. But it's that vulnerability that will inspire you to press on when you otherwise might not.

You've got goals, right? Share them with someone.

## -76-
## I Respect Your Opinion

Your ability to form an opinion is God given. And your right to freely share it is guaranteed by the Constitution. While you have these rights and abilities, you need to remember that your opinion is yours and no one else's.

Likewise, you need to know that if you attempt to force your opinions on others or even aggressively advocate them, in a weird sort of way, you violate their trust in you.

Remember, these people have opinions too. And you should be accepting of that. This is not to suggest that you need to concede your position on issues or ideas. Accepting is merely the action of understanding that others have a different perspective and respecting that they have a right to it.

You don't have to agree on the issue. But you can agree that you come to the situation from different perspectives. Then move forward and look for common ground.

## -77-
## Option B Giving

In her book *Option B: Facing Adversity, Building Resilience, and Finding Joy*, Facebook COO Sheryl Sandberg encourages that in seeking to help others you should avoid making blanket offers like:

"If there is anything I can do for you, let me know." OR, "What can I do for you?"

This is especially true when the person you're looking to help is dealing with hardship or tragedy. While well intended, these open gestures add to the person's burden, as it puts the onus on them to think of something you can do (and in times of adversity they don't need one more thing to think about or one more decision to make).

Rather, your efforts will be more appreciated if you go with something like:

"Would it be helpful if I did THIS for you?" OR "I'm going to do THIS for you. If that's a problem, or if something else is more pressing, let me know. Otherwise, consider THIS done."

## -78-
## Tell Me More

No one likes conflict. It's generally human nature to avoid it. But as much as you look to avoid it, at times it finds you, right?

Communication consultant, Kay Coughlin offers a way to de-escalate most any tense situation and it boils down to three simple syllables: Tell me more.

The owner of Facilitator on Fire, Coughlin shares that, "When someone corners you to talk about your job choices, or grills your girlfriend about her ex-husband's Facebook profile, or tells you how disappointed they are with your cooking, you can *always* choose to reply, 'Tell me more.'"

And she encourages you to say it as many times as you need to. It's a diplomatic and friendly way to let someone talk out their issue. The beauty is, however, that you never have to pretend to agree or even offer your own opinion. Just let them tell you more.

## -79-
## Valuable Rocks

Gold miners don't stuff their sacks with any old rock. No. They're selective. They choose only those rocks that they perceive to have value.

To effectively "mine" a networking event, you should take a similar approach. It's not a matter of amassing lots and lots of connections. Rather, focus on finding value. In the long run, a few quality connections will benefit you more than a pocket full of business cards.

Any gathering of people – a party, tradeshow, or business after-hours - can be a networking event. And any of these you can mine. Use these as opportunities to wisely expand the base of your connections with a few great people upon which you can build relationships.

Then, from these valuable rocks, you open yourself to being connected to other great contacts, invaluable information, and opportunities that can make your day, week, or year.

## -80-
## Focus Attention on Others

For just a moment, consider the very real possibility that a big reason you aren't getting everything you want in life is because you're too focused on getting everything you want in life. Think about it.

Anything and everything you want absolutely will require the assistance of others. For any of it, you'll need connections. Others can generate those for you. You'll need information and opportunities. The people around you can bring those forth too.

But to receive the assistance of others, you need to contribute to their worlds. And you can't possibly do that if you're too focused on getting everything you want.

So, to get all you want in life, stop. Take a step back. And focus your attention on others. Ask yourself what you can bring to their world. When you have answers, act upon them. You'll find that in time you'll get more of what you want when you help others get more of what they want.

## -81-
## Awareness Quotient

Super connector, speaker and social capital consultant, Terry Bean shares in his book *Be Connected*:

"Be aware of your surroundings and the plethora of things going on around you at any point in time. Be aware of the opportunities and signs that present themselves to you all day long. Be aware of your surroundings and all the sights, sounds and smells. Be aware of the impact that your actions can and do have on those around you. And be aware of the impact that the actions of others have on you. Be aware of what's being said in conversations by listening intently and not focusing on formulating a response."

Bean refers to this as your Awareness Quotient and he defines it as being in tune with the flow of your life. So, stop and become a little more aware today. As he says, "Love the moments you live, and you will live the moments you love."

## -82-
## Business Card Tips From Afar

Whenever you have an opportunity to hand out your business card, follow a practice of Far Eastern countries: Use both hands in delivering it. This gives the subtle but important impression that your business card is something very valuable.

Along those same lines, when someone gives you their business card, don't put it away right away. Rather, keep it in your hands for a while and study it carefully. As you do, talk to them about it or use it to segue into a conversation, such as, "How did you come up with that business name?"

If you take an interest in their card, they are more likely to take an interest in yours. And, if they take more interest in your card, they will probably remember you that much more. And isn't that the point of your business card in the first place?

## -83-
## A Spirit of Service

Networking is about serving others. The more you serve others, the more you put into the world. And the more you put into the world, the more things that will come back to you. To this end, here is a thought.

No matter how bad off you might have it, the reality is that someone likely has it worse. Therefore, there should never be a shortage of people you can serve.

With that, a simple key to infusing a spirit of service in your life is to look around for someone to serve. They are there. People needing encouragement. People needing a little direction. People needing things you can help them with.

When you find one, understand their struggles. Then from here, you can certainly find a means of easing their heartache or lifting them up – even if only temporarily. And just like that you are serving the world around you.

## -84-
## Orchestrate Relationships

In his book *Who Do You Need To Meet?*, author Rob Thomas share a secret to his networking success.

"My intention while meeting with someone for the first time is to think about others who have something in common or might be interested in the person across the table from me. I like to orchestrate relationships between quality people who may be able to benefit from each other's offerings, expertise or connections."

Thomas goes on to share that he truly enjoys connecting people who might never have otherwise met. Further, he gets a sense of real fulfillment when sometimes these connections cultivate lasting business relationships and can even become friends.

So, you meet new people every day. And you already know a bunch. To what extent are you orchestrating relationships? Could you be doing a better at initiating new business relationships? What friendship might you be able to inspire? What might this do for your networking success?

## -85-
## The Whole Journey

Late in the championship game, down by four, within mere yards of the endzone and only time left for this one last play, the veteran quarterback drops back to pass.

It's been amazing. The QB's season-long heroics got his team into the playoffs. And then he somehow willed them to the championship. Finally, he almost single-handedly mounted a 20-point comeback and got them downfield in position to win.

In the end zone, is a wide-open receiver. Unfortunately, however, the star quarterback put too on the pass. It sails incomplete. The game is lost. The season is over.

One fan screams, "Oh my God ... I can't believe he missed. Anyone could have made that."

To which another fan calmly remarks, "Yes, anyone could have made that pass. But there is only one man in the world who could have gotten this team in this position to have this opportunity."

The point: Before you criticize the failures of others, consider the merits of their whole journey.

## -86-
## One Size Does Not Fit All

In business, you're not a one-trick pony. That is, there is lots to you as a business professional and you serve clients in many, many ways. As such, don't limit yourself to a single 30–second commercial that becomes tired and seemingly trite in time.

Rather, start by taking the time to develop a variety of small business introductions for yourself. Work one up for each aspect on your aspect of your business.

Then with that foundation, work up some variations on those. Make some that involve short anecdotes. Make some that are cute and entertaining. Have others that play well in a more professional setting.

Don't limit yourself. Be so prepared with material, that you appear to come up with great introduction on the fly. Ones that are not just engaging, but more importantly productive.

## -87-
## The Sun Still Shines

In his book *The Power of Optimism*, corporate psychologist and motivational speaker Tim Shurr reminds readers that "even on the darkest, cloudiest, rainiest day, the sun is still shining – you just can't see it." He continues that in reality, you're just not looking for it.

So, when times are tough, and problems appear overwhelming (and everyone has these days) know that solutions are right there. Right there within reach. But you have to take a deep breath, step back and relax, and start to look for them.

And as you look trust that it's not a question of "if" you will find the solution. Rather, it's a matter of where you'll find the solution and what it will be.

So next time you find yourself embroiled in a day that feels dark, cloudy, and rainy, remember that somewhere around you is the answer that will serve as some sunshine. You just need to look for it.

## -88-
## Initiating Contact

When you're at networking events, it is simply up to you to initiate contact. That is, making contact is 100% your obligation, if you want a productive experience.

You can, however, easily make it happen with three simple steps.

One. Make meaningful eye contact with people, where you look at them and they look you back in the eye. There is nothing strange about this. It is completely human.

Two. With eye contact established, smile. This is not a forced smile, but a genuine "it is good to see you" smile. Chances are, human nature will kick in and they will smile back.

Three. With that eye contact and a smile, simply say, "hello." They may say "hello" in return, or they may say nothing.

Whatever the case, it was your objective (as well as sole obligation) to initiate contact. You've done that. Congratulations!

## -89-
## Network Pyramid Capstones

In the 1960s, Yale researcher Stanley Milgram adopted the phrase "six degrees of separation". This phrase came about because, on average, there were a half-dozen intermediaries involved in the delivery of packets of information from randomly selected people in Omaha to a stockbroker in Boston.

Interestingly, however, while the packets originated from numerous random points, the final step of their delivery came from only a handful of people. From this, Milgram concluded that a very small number of people are linked to everyone else in just a few steps, and the rest of us are linked to the world through them.

To find these "super connectors" in your life, write down the names of 50 random contacts and trace them back to how you were introduced. A pattern will emerge showing that a large percentage of your contacts likely originated from relatively few individuals.

These people are called network pyramid capstones, and they are instrumental in your world. Devote time and energy to building your relationship with them.

## -90-
## Big Impact From Small Things

To build a great following of wonderful people, you need to devote time and energy to helping others. Giving referrals. Making introductions. Sharing information. Generally, adding value.

Sure, it might seem like that Herculean effort is the most noteworthy. The bigger the help, the bigger the splash in someone else's life, right? However, as word of mouth referral expert Matt Wards reminds us: "Sometimes it's doing something small for someone that really makes a big impact."

What Ward implies is that you're not always in a position to share referrals that make someone's quarter or information that alters the landscape of someone's business. You are, however, always able to do something. Write a note. Call to just check in. Offer encouragement.

While these small things can seem inconsequential, you never know what impact they can bring. And sometimes the impact can be really big. So, commit to doing something small today. And see what it leads to tomorrow.

## -91-
## 90 Seconds of Courage

No doubt, you want more. More money. A nicer car. Improved opportunities. Greater understanding and insight. Additional wonderful contacts upon which to build your business and career. You want more.

And that's okay. You're no different from everyone else on the planet. Wanting more is a fundamental principle of the human condition. Everyone wants more. The only people who consistently get it, however, are those with the courage to go after it.

Courage! The courage to confidently walk into a new networking event for the first time. Courage! The courage to engage a complete stranger in conversation. Courage! The courage to quietly listen, even though you have much to say. Courage! The courage to, in time, ask for what you need in terms of contacts, information and opportunities.

If you want more, it takes courage. You'd be completely amazed as to what awaits you on the other side of 90 seconds of courage.

## -92-
## Creating a Referral Machine

If you're in business, you want referrals. After all, this is the best place to be: where others are directing clients to you. Just because you want this, however, doesn't mean that you get it. To create this referral machine, you must build it.

To do so, the onus is on you to establish relationships. After all people do business with and refer business to those that they know, like and trust.

As you build those relationships, you must also empower your network to not just understand what you do. In addition, you need to help these people to be able to both recognize opportunities for you as well as talk about you to others.

Finally, to maintain this referral machine, you must remain in continual contact with your network to cultivate these relationships. This is the grease that ensures the referrals flow.

Yes, this all takes work, but the rewards far outpace the effort.

## -93-
## The Formula of Trust

On the NetworkWise blog, social architect Adam Connors shares that the formula for building trust in any professional network is as simple as providing value over an extended period of time. In short, time plus value equals trust.

To offer value, Connors states that "You could comment on and share recent blog post. Or give advice on a project they're working on." But Connors then goes on to acknowledge that there are so many other ways you can bring value, like being a good listener, being a mentor, or just being there for them in general.

As for time, Connors encourages you to make time to spend with your network, whether over a meal, just talking on the phone, or maybe volunteering together, as contact alone serves to build trust.

But more importantly, Connors chides you to ensure that you follow through on your commitments or promises. Consistently doing this demonstrates that you're reliable, which is just another word for trustworthy.

## -94-
## A Lesson From Master Networkers

Some people are master networkers. They seem to effortlessly establish, develop, and maintain a framework of individuals comprised of family, friends, co-workers, business colleagues and even competitors.

How do they do this? The reality is that master networkers are not necessarily harder working than others. They are not necessarily any more educated. And it has nothing to do with their social status, appearance, or luck. The difference is the manner and approach in which master networkers interact with their networks.

Masters know that they need to be more than simply acquainted with their network. Masters look for a deeper relationship with those they associate with. In summary, master networkers strive to develop a mutual sense of knowing, liking and trusting amongst their contacts.

Masters are aware – at least on some level of consciousness – that the notion of 'know, like and trust' is the key to forging a powerful and productive relationship. And that is a simple lesson you can take from the master networker.

## -95-
## Social Media Success

Social media ... like LinkedIn, Facebook, Instagram, and Twitter ... has created a whole new experience for networking. Now, if you're looking to find success networking on social media, there is no magic. There are no secret formulas or short cuts. The key is to follow these three important steps.

One - get your account set up or, if you're already set up, expand your usage to be more effective. Two - schedule time to take a little action each day. And three - commit to keeping after it.

Yep, it's that simple. Sure, there is a lot there and much to master and learn. Nothing, however, says you need to climb the learning curve in one day, one month or even one year. Even the most proficient users of social media find that they are continually learning new things.

Besides, no one is judging you on your proficiency using social media. They are only judging you on the value you bring. So, get started.

## -96-
## Open and Accepting

In her book *The Connector's Advantage*, consultant Michelle Lederman reveals seven mindsets that will lead to having a more impactful and influential network. The first mindset she encourages is being 'open and accepting.'

She shares "To be open and accepting means you recognize and accept the good and bad aspects about yourself and, just as importantly, you accept the good and bad sides of others."

As Lederman implies, to be best networked, you only need be yourself. That persona will serve you well long term. Being someone else only leaves you continually on edge as you try to keep up the ruse.

At the same time, allow others the comfort of knowing, they can be themselves. No matter what rung of success they're on, it doesn't really matter. All that is important is offering help to get them to the next.

Remember, through an open and accepting mindset, bad can be turned to good. And the good become better.

## -97-
## Conversation Starters

Big things come from small talk. There is little argument with that. The almost non-sensical conversation that occupies the first few minutes of any encounter sets the tone for how the rest of the interaction will go.

Knowing this, it's important that you're ready with a handful of conversation starters. These are comments and inquiries intended to get others sharing and nothing more. Some examples could include:

"I'm not familiar with your business. What can you tell me about it?"

Or, "Based on your accent, you're not from here. Where are you from and how did you end up here?"

Or, "This weather is something else. How does it impact your operations?"

Sure, these are a series of everyday comments followed by a related question. But that's the point. Getting a conversation started doesn't have to be a science. It just has to invite a chat.

By the way, "Did you happen to see the game last night?"

## -98-
## Ending the Drought

In 2011, with virtually no time remaining on the game clock, Ryan Elmquist, the all-time leading scorer for the California Institute of Technology men's basketball program, made two free throws. In so doing, he broke a tie with the Occidental College Tigers and ensured a victory. More importantly, Elmquist ended a 310-game, 26-year winning drought for the Cal Tech Beavers.

Chances are you've never gone two and a half decades without a win, whether in sports, business, or life. No doubt, however, you been involved in a drought. You know. That patch where nothing seems to go right. Where none of your ideas are accepted. Where promotion after promotion seem to pass you by. Where you can't seem to catch a break on anything.

Just as no one can expect to win every encounter, you should know that no matter how things have been going, your day is coming. Whatever the circumstance, keep after it. Eventually, you will break through.

## -99-
## Influence Through Consensus

As Brian Ahearn shares in his book *Influence People*, "When people are unsure how to act in certain situations, they tend to look to others to see how they should respond."

With this insight, if you're trying to influence people in your network, you can nudge them in your direction simply by reminding them that there are other people who are already doing what you're asking of them.

In fact, you can accentuate your influence by telling people that those who are already doing what you're asking are just like them. As Ahearn shares, "We are especially motivated to move with the crowd when that crowd is just like us. We feel more confident following along."

What Ahearn implies is don't ask someone to do something you wouldn't. Rather, you're better off asking them to do something that others just like them are already doing.

## -100-
## Tickle Someone

The most effect way of tickling someone is to sneak up on them and do it without them knowing it's coming. While I don't advocate doing this to a stranger, you likely have a loved one in your life where this is useful advice.

Just like tickling someone else, your acts of altruism are most effective when you sneak up on the person to present it.

Your spouse or significant other is romantically moved when you shower them with cards and flowers when they least expect them.

Your compliments have a special meaning when you give them without any sort of solicitation.

And, the referrals you give, the information you share, and the business contacts you create for others go from ordinary gestures to extraordinary acts of altruism when you do them without any sort of prompting. So, don't wait to be asked to do anything. Just sneak up and do it without them knowing it's coming.

## -101-
## Seven-Second Delay

Have you ever met someone only to completely forgot their name moments later? Who hasn't? On the full Networking Rx podcast, Lynne Franklin – author of the book *Getting Others To Do What You Want* – shared a simple tactic to ensure that this never happens to you ... well, at least not again.

Franklin advised that when you meet someone for the first time that you occupy the first portion of the encounter with an almost nonsensical exchange. Like, "This coffee is great. Did you try it?" Or "Have you been to this event before?"

She shares that during this initial segment, your subconscious mind is flooded with information. Their hair. Their tie. Most everything about them. It's not in a great state to remember their name, anyway. So, chances are you don't.

If, however, you hold off asking their name, the seven-second delay will better ensure that you remember it.

**There you have it—101 essays. But we wanted to offer a bonus essay. Before we do, if you're interested in exploring other books, content, and programs by Frank Agin, visit frankagin.com or simply search "Frank Agin" on whatever platform you use to get great content.**

## -102-
## Be A Galactic Anthropologist

In his Thinks Again series Wharton Business School psychology professor Dr. Adam Grant shares advice he was given for dealing with people who have dramatically different views:

"When you find out someone holds beliefs that you see as wrong or offensive, you think of yourself as a galactic anthropologist who's just discovered alien life. You say to yourself, "Wow, what a fascinating specimen!" Instead of pure outrage at their opinions, you start to get curious about how they arrived at those opinions—and what would motivate them to change them."

You don't need Grant to know that the world has always had a wide variety of views and opinions. And with 24-hour news and social media they can come at you literally at the speed of light.

But by becoming curious, you can transform angry into understanding. And in so doing you position yourself to become more constructive in your approach to the world.

## About The Author

Frank Agin is president of AmSpirit Business Connections, which empowers entrepreneurs, sales representatives, and professionals to become successful and gain more referrals through networking.

He also shares information and insights on professional relationships, business networking and best practices for generating referrals on his Networking Rx podcast and through various professional programs.

Finally, Frank is the author of several books, including *Foundational Networking: Building Know, Like & Trust to Create a Life of Extraordinary Success*. See all his books and programs at frankagin.com. You can reach him at frankagin@amspirit.com.

www.ingramcontent.com/pod-product-compliance
Lightning Source LLC
Chambersburg PA
CBHW040757220326
41597CB00029BB/4967
*9781967521111*